# BACK HOME

## LIVING WITH CHANGE AFTER TIME ABROAD

CHRISTINE SCHUPPENER
JOCHEN SCHUPPENER

# BACK HOME
## LIVING WITH CHANGE AFTER TIME ABROAD

# INHALT

## Leaving
### THE RIGHT TIMING

14    Does Time Abroad Even Make Sense?

16    The Right Time for Moving

19    Relationship and Children When Leaving

24    Celebrating the Farewell

32    What is Normal in the Process of Saying, „Goodbye"?

34    Is There a Wrong Way to Say, „Goodbye"?

## The Move
### KING OF CHAOS?

40    Loss of Status

43    Chaos and Disruption

45    The Move–King of Chaos?

47    Worries About the Future

---

ISBN 9783741208935

© 2016 Jochen und Christine Schuppener
Production and Publisher: BOD—Books on Demand, Norderstedt
Original title: *Rückkehr aus dem Ausland* © 2015

All rights reserved. No part of this book may be reproduced in any form without permission in writing from the authors, except in the case of brief quotations embodied in critical articles or reviews.

Translation: Karen Alberg, Michael Zabel
Author Portrait: Sonia Epple
Cover, typography and illustrations: Daniel Zabel

## INTRODUCTION

For many years we have assisted people in their return process to their homeland. Time and time again we realized how important a well-planned process is for a successful reintegration experience.

It all started with our own return after having spent eight years abroad. From observing other former expats we knew that reintegration does not simply happen. We observed that some had real challenges coming back to their homeland. On the other hand, we had received much support from friends towards the end of our stay. They asked us questions to reflect upon our time abroad. A good farewell with small, but significant rituals was very helpful for our entire family. We also realized that our children's "home" was actually in the host nation, abroad. Germany was the country where Grandma and Grandpa lived. The people there were quite different.

Also, we had changed. We were not aware of those changes, which usually became apparent with misunderstandings and unexpected conflicts. Our experiences developed our desire to support others in similar situations. Since that time, we have been able to support expats from all over the world in this important stage so they, too, could experience successful reintegration to their homelands.

An intense period of life abroad lies behind you. You experienced many milestones—some positive, and some challenging. And now you are heading back. Through our consultations and seminars as intercultural counselors, we try to emphasize how the valuable experiences from the previous years as an expat can be included in the very important process of returning to the homeland. It is our desire to encourage you and to give you practical advice as you embark on this journey.

We want to thank those whom we have been able to support over the past years. It has been a privilege to be part of this important process with each of you. Many ideas for this book came as responses to our clients' needs.

When returning home after many intense years abroad, many people think, "No problem, I know what's up. This will be quite easy, unlike my departure when I did not have a clue."

However, the reintegration of expats poses a problem to many companies and organizations.

While most companies offer in-service and training for preparing for the stay abroad, it is hard to find reintegration programs. Only 14% of surveyed companies have a formal repatriation strategy.

The return to the home country is often characterized by a feeling of being somehow in the wrong place, of not fitting in, and of being like a stranger. Usually questions start coming up shortly after the initial joy of returning "home," such as:

- How do I find my place at work and in society?
- What do I need now? What do my spouse and our children need?
- Does anyone understand me?

A good reintegration starts before the actual physical return. Those who start thinking about this process early enough create the best foundation for a successful return and reintegration.

Above all, the experiences gained abroad can enrich one's life, giving new perspectives and energy. But that does not happen automatically.

This book will give you a new perspective about the dynamics of return home. You will find many handy hints and practical ideas for a successful reintegration.

80% of those who go abroad travel with their spouse, and more than 60% travel with their family; therefore, we also will give ideas to support your relationships, both with your spouse and your children.

We hope you enjoy reading, pondering, and applying this book to your unique situation.

We are grateful for feedback on this important subject. Please feel free to share your experiences and questions to info@schuppener-global-transitions.com

*Jochen and Christine Schuppener*

● ○ ○ ○

# Leaving

## THE RIGHT TIMING

| | |
|---|---|
| 14 | Does Time Abroad Even Make Sense? |
| 16 | The Right Time for Moving |
| 19 | Relationship and Children When Leaving |
| 24 | Celebrating the Farewell |
| 32 | What is Normal in the Process of Saying, „Goodbye"? |
| 34 | Is There a Wrong Way to Say, „Goodbye"? |

Feeling at home in a foreign country! That sounds really good. After some initial uncertainties about cultural "do's and don`ts," you navigated your way through. You recognized that some rules from your country of origin, do not apply here. Of course you still drop a brick ones in while, but that is part of being here. You came to appreciate the new culture, you know where to get what you need, and you became accustomed to the language. Everything feels normal—somewhat like home. Does that sound familiar to you?

Or did you find it more difficult? You never really understood the people here, and you usually felt like an outsider. You are glad that it is over now.

Or was it more like this? The locals were not the problem, but rather you had trouble with your international colleagues. To which culture should you adapt? You preferred the company of your native-language community.

It could also be that you did not want to return „home" at all. It was your organization or company, the government authorities, or the age of your children that forced you to come back.

## DOES TIME ABROAD EVEN MAKE SENSE?

Experiences abroad are valuable. Studies show that time spent abroad has positive effects on everyone involved—for you, your spouse, and your children (who accompany 60% of those who go abroad). This is why we often address families in this book.

You already know that moving can be a time of chaos—suitcases, boxes, arguments, children out of control...

That is one thing, but beyond that our emotions are also in turmoil.

People describe having mixed feelings, a roller coaster of emotions. The stress level is slowly, but constantly increasing, and at some point our nerves usually snap.

Is there a right or a wrong time to plan the move? When does moving make sense—and when does it not?

**TIPS:**

Here are some questions you should ask yourself:

- How often have I already moved?
- Which aspects were most strenuous and stressful for me?
- What helped me then the most?
- What helps me relax in the chaos?
- What time of the year is moving the easiest for me? When is it the most stressful?
- If you have a spouse, are both of you in agreement on moving?

You should also consider the length of your time abroad. How long are you planning or required to stay abroad? Do you have a temporary contract, or do you have greater flexibility?

The longer you stayed abroad, the more challenges can arise when returning. Procedures and technology change. That also applies to a return into your previous work environment. Company hierarchy may change; your former peer might now be your superior. The company staff may have changed, and a new boss might have a completely different leadership style.

Dynamics in your social circles and organizations will have changed. Family structures will no longer be the same. Friends will have married, and other relationships will have ended. New children have been born. Acquaintances will have moved. Even at your fitness center you may have new staff and a new trainer.

The right time for moving must be chosen carefully. However, we do not always have the luxury of choosing it independently.

Some may be forced to end their stay abroad early for any number of reasons. Maybe there have been political changes in the host country, the visa cannot be renewed, or one actually gets deported. It could also be that the sending organization closes down their branch or ends their foreign engagement. In some cases, an evacuation might even be necessary for safety.

In those cases the move will not be as easy to orchestrate as if it had been prepared for over an extended period of time. The emotional challenges are intensified. Under these circumstances, receiving support from a specialist will be beneficial.

## RELATIONSHIP AND CHILDREN WHEN LEAVING

### CHILD DEVELOPMENTAL STAGES

Children generally develop a sense of order at the age of two or three. They learn where shoes in the house usually are left, where dishes and clothing belong, and that doors are meant to be closed.

They recognize daily routines and develop their own, bringing an understanding of orderly routines. That understanding lays an important foundation for appreciating structure later in life. An infant growing up in a host country will develop a sense of order according to its current surroundings. A child's sense of routine and stability gets easily confused during a move. Even as an adult, you will most likely also lose your routine during the moving process. Daily schedules are interrupted. If you are looking for documents, clothing, and shoes, how can you maintain a routine for your children?

Social contacts and educational routines play an important role in the life of an elementary school-aged child. Children between six and ten years are very opinionated about what defines right and wrong behavior. The culture and expressions of their host country have often become normal. Learning new skills, such as reading and writing, are paramount. Friends become more and more important. Their relationships with teachers and other authority figures are often intense and emotional.

**TIPS:**

Try to maintain some kind of a routine as long as possible before moving, and take steps to implement a new routine as quickly as possible after completing the move.

### IDENTITY CRISIS WITH TEENAGERS

A planned move from the host country to the homeland will have a profound effect on a teen's friendships and recreational activities. Adolescents define themselves through their peers. Hobbies and interests are important as they find their identity. A move to a different country will significantly impact a teenager because his whole world is being turned upside down. Psychologists have discovered that such moves often result in teen depression.

Teenagers, especially, try to separate themselves from their parents as they try to find their own identity. The values and rules of society help an adolescent to find out who he is. An intercultural move can lead to confusion and identity crisis. When a teen becomes overwhelmed, it may lead to withdrawal and feelings of rejection, and possibly even depression.

> **TIPS:**
>
> Relevant questions for farewells with children
> - How often did our child move already? How did he react?
> - During which developmental stage did we move?
> - What obstacles is our child already facing at the moment?
> - Do we know people with similar experiences? Can we talk about similar experiences?
> - What helps our child cope with stress and chaos?
> - What do we need to consider when it comes to his education?
> - What academic challenges does our child experience? How does the curriculum here compare with the curriculum back home?
> - How will the move affect our child's support system?

Routine and repetition provide security. That becomes especially helpful during a move, when changing circumstances lead to insecurity. What had been normal for an extended period suddenly changes. This can include things such as work procedures and schedules, colleagues, friends, and hobbies. For children it includes education as well as daily routines. Ahead lies great uncertainty. Any positive routines which can be maintained will provide stability. For some this might be a quiet cup of coffee in the morning while reading the news. For others it might be keeping a journal or going for a run. Families might continue the routines of sharing a meal, playing a game, or reading bedtime-stories. Spiritual routines, including prayer or meditation, become especially important to many. Which routines do you find comforting? What steps can you take to maintain them?

## INCLUDING TEENAGERS IN THE DECISION-MAKING PROCESS

Try to include older children and teenagers in decision making, even if it is more time consuming. When your children take ownership of the process, they will become partners in the transition. Your relationship with your spouse is another crucial aspect in providing stability for your children.

## STRENGTHENING YOUR RELATIONSHIP BEFORE THE MOVE

Rarely is anything more important for children than their parents' relationship. Your children are facing many challenges. They will be better able to cope if they are confident that their parents love each other, solve problems together, and deal with conflict in a healthy way.

## COOPERATING: THE GAME CHANGER

Cooperation in your relationship is a game changer. Both of you are challenged and often tested to your limit. The stronger your relationship is, the better you can master the challenges you are facing. But that does not simply happen.

**TIPS:**

Questions you may ask each other as a couple

- How good is the quality of our communication? When do we communicate most effectively?
- Do we invest time into our relationship?
- How do we solve conflicts?
- Do we find it hard to forgive each other?
- Do we have a fulfilling sex life? What steps can we take to strengthen our relationship?
- Do we express our love in ways that our partner truly feels loved?*
- What builds my spouse up?
- How do we create an environment to facilitate open and honest communication?

Good communication with everyone involved is the key to a successful move. The stronger and more trusting the relationships within a marriage and family are, the better able you will be to have a successful transition. Make it a priority to strengthen your relationships before you move.

---

* *An excellent resource is *The Five Love Languages* by Gary Chapman (additional editions focusing on children—*The Five Love Languages of Children*, singles, men, or families are available). *Nonviolent Communication* by Marshall B. Rosenberg is another great resource

## CELEBRATING THE FAREWELL

You are now headed back home. Your departure date is set, and your time in your host country is coming to an end. You have accomplished goals, experienced much, and learned throughout the process. You came to love new people and places, and mastered a new lifestyle with all its challenges. Maybe you are not fully convinced. Many things seem surreal. Why not take fifteen minutes and write down all the people from whom you have learned, the ones who enriched you? What do you enjoy about your host country? Which parts of the culture do you appreciate? I am sure many things will come to mind, and those deserve to be celebrated properly. In order to enjoy the farewell, you should keep a few things in mind.

### THE RAFT-STRATEGY

A raft is made to float down a river. Returning from abroad according to Dave Pollock can be compared to a trip on a raft. For the raft to arrive safely, it must be durable. The RAFT-Strategy can support you in the process of saying goodbye.

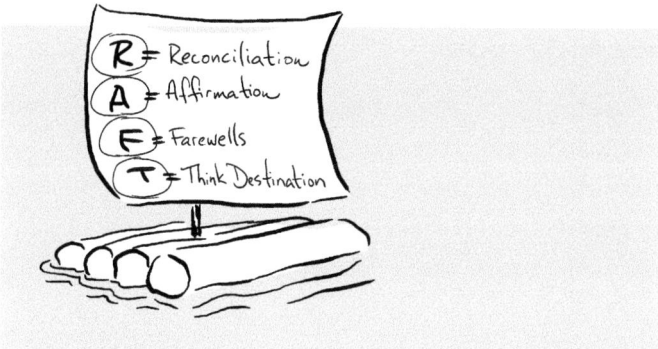

- R–Reconciliation
- A–Affirmation
- F–Farewells
- T–Think Destination

## R–RECONCILIATION

During a foreign assignment, misunderstandings and conflicts can arise at work, among your team of colleagues, or within the international community. Sometimes you may be tempted to avoid the issues. You may think, "I'm leaving anyway and I will not have to see him anymore." That is true, but it may leave a bitter aftertaste when you are thousands of miles away. Consider making one more attempt to solve the problem? The goodbye-phase is a good time to reconcile.

Reconciliation is the first very important "log" for floating down the river of farewells.

**A–AFFIRMATION**

Affirmation and appreciation mean that you express your gratitude for what you have experienced. You did not enjoy some things, yet they were valuable learning opportunities. Despite the normal sadness of saying farewell, your goodbye party can be more than a "memorial service."

**F–FAREWELLS**

Farewell means saying "goodbye" in a good and healthy way to coworkers, neighbors, and friends. However, it goes beyond saying "bye" to people and includes animals and places. Much has become significant over the past years. It may include special wardrobe choices, or the warm morning sunshine, or the spicy regional food. Surely you enjoyed special places, perhaps a significant vacation destination or your favorite spot under the palm tree in the front yard. Taking time to say goodbye to animals is especially important to children, whether it be their pet or the humming birds in the front window. Some aspects demand a quiet goodbye, and others a more boisterous one. For both adults and children, an improper farewell may leave an unpleasant sense of unfinished business. Your soul may "refuse" to walk towards something new.

> **TIPS:**
>
> Try to make a list of people you want to spend time with eight weeks before your departure. Take pictures of animals and places that are important to you. Good parting rituals are fundamental for a durable RAFT and a nice farewell celebration.

## FORCED FAREWELLS

Leaving your host country very suddenly—perhaps due to political unrest, safety issues, or visa concerns —can be emotionally stressful. If you desire to return at some point, it is advised to do so if at all possible. A professional debriefing may help you better process the entire situation emotionally.

Debriefing involves reflecting upon an experience and thereby gaining a new perspective and new energy for the future. Debriefing also involves confronting difficult experiences, or maybe even frightening or traumatic events, in order to experience resolution where it is necessary. Debriefing helps to:
- reduce emotional and physical stress
- prevent "burnouts"
- facilitate the return and reintegration process

## T–THINK DESTINATION

If you have done some realistic thinking about what is waiting for you downstream, back "home," you can begin your journey more relaxed. Many people neglect this and often have romanticized memories of their life before they left. They tell their children stories about the vast opportunities available in their homeland. Some of that is valid, but please do not forget that your "home" is not the same as it was before you left. Some describe spending a year abroad is as if one has been gone for two. It means you have embraced a new world in your year away, and you have adapted and changed; however, time hasn't stopped in your old "home." Things have changed. Your company has introduced new routines and adopted new technology. Some coworkers may have changed employment. Society is also constantly changing. While the thought that one year away is the equivalent to two years of change may not be entirely realistic, there is truth to the statement. Whoever thinks that everything will still be the same back home may be disappointed.

The people back at home often demonstrate great interest while the expat is abroad. When visiting, they often ask questions. Foreign aid workers, particularly, are sometimes viewed with idealized curiosity. They are admired for their foreign assignment, which is often perceived as risky and perhaps even dangerous. Surprisingly, this often is not the case when they finally come back. The returning expat was not expecting that—and how could he?

The homecoming can quickly lead to disillusionment if not viewed in a realistic way. Good preparation will keep you from being too disappointed.

Some organizations and companies offer a "home trip" prior to the actual return, providing a helpful opportunity to scope things out. Families with children find visiting a new school may be beneficial. The familiarity gives their students a confidence boost when actually starting at the new school. Homeschooling can provide a good routine especially in those very intense weeks of transition.

**TIPS:**

> One fun way of getting ready for returning to your home country may be looking at trends. What are the latest fashions? What are the newest catch phrases? What are the popular TV shows? Use the internet to look up opportunities and activities in your homeland. These considerations, as well as the questions in the beginning of the chapter, will help you get the final log of your raft ready to go.

## TIPS FOR A FAREWELL PARTY

Let's have a look at the practical preparation for your farewell party. Start by asking the important "W"-questions early enough—When? Who? What? Where?

If you compile your guest list together a month or two early, you may find some guests with whom you want to spend more time or do something special. You will rarely have time for meaningful one-on-one conversations at the celebration.

> **TIPS:**
>
> Here are some more practical ideas:
>
> Memory album
>
> - Ask for personal contributions (maybe a funny, exciting, or special shared experience)
> - Take a photo of every guest
> - Compile the pictures and the stories in one album

A memory album ensures you receive a personal keepsake. Invite your friends out to dinner, perhaps in your favorite restaurant or at your house. The size of your gathering can be determined by your personal preference. If you have children, ask them how they imagine their party to be. Needs may vary among siblings; some children find a personal party to be too emotionally intense, while it is important to others.

### GIFTS

Choose goodbye gifts thoughtfully. A present can express gratitude and appreciation in a meaningful way. It may be very important to children that they have the opportunity to present a carefully chosen gift.

### BALLOONS

"Sky balloons" in Southeast Asia and helium balloons in other cultures may be used to attach thoughts of gratitude or good wishes before releasing them. Use these or other creative opportunities from your local culture.

### TRIPS TOGETHER

A trip together to an especially beautiful or meaningful place can be a nice connective experience during the farewell process. Perhaps you will choose to attend a sporting event or a concert with people who have become important to you during your stay. A visit to a special restaurant with friends could also be an experience that you will remember fondly.

### MUSIC AND DANCE

Have you learned any local dances? If you have, you will want to incorporate those into your farewell. Music and dance do an excellent job conveying emotion and are a great support tool in the farewell process.

### GOODBYE SPEECH

A farewell speech gives you a special opportunity to express your thankfulness. Do not miss out on that chance.

The memories of your foreign assignment depend largely on the farewell. Take your time with the process and end your stay positively in every aspect, both professionally and socially.

## WHAT IS NORMAL IN THE PROCESS OF SAYING „GOODBYE"?

As soon as you recognize the end of your time abroad, a new phase begins. Almost unnoticeably, you begin distancing yourself internally. Often it starts by looking at the calendar and realizing that a certain future event will take place without you because you will no longer be in the country. Beginning to disengage yourself from current relationships is a very natural reaction.

### MENTALLY DONE PACKING

"I am mentally done packing." That is a good description for what happens emotionally, even if you still have three to four months before you actually begin to pack. In your mind you are living between two worlds. The short-term planning takes place in your host nation, yet you are making decisions every day which will affect your future in your homeland.

## DISTANCING

To a certain degree, distancing helps protect us from emotional pain. Farewells are mostly unpleasant and painful, so in order to protect ourselves we tend to withdraw somewhat from our relationships. In some respects that makes the actual farewell easier, but that is only partially true.

Meanwhile, the people who have become close to you are going through a similar process. They are also beginning to distance themselves, both internally and perhaps even outwardly. It is difficult emotionally when coworkers, friends, neighbors, and your children's classmates slowly begin to withdraw. Please do not take this distancing personal; it is not meant that way.

## YOU DO NOT SEEM TO BE WANTED ANYMORE

Why is that so? Yesterday you were best friends or great colleagues who got along well, and suddenly you sense a cold shoulder in some relationships. "You are leaving anyway," some might say, or others might not even verbalize anything; however, you recognize that others are excluding you. You no longer get asked for input regarding decisions. Your children might not get invited to birthday parties anymore, even though they are not leaving for three months.

That is part of the farewell process. Being aware of this dynamic makes it easier to cope.

### MAKING GOODBYES EASIER

Just as you are starting to say goodbye and loosen connections to make the actual farewell easier, your colleagues must do the same. They have to think about the time after your parting. What will happen after you are gone? What can happen? What needs to be done? All of that is a normal part of the process.

Sometimes this withdrawal does not happen and the relationship continues until the very last minute. In these circumstances, the entire emotional stress of saying goodbye may hit you once you board the plane.

Distancing yourself and being excluded is a normal and very important aspect of saying goodbye, even if it is unpleasant. Be prepared for it.

## IS THERE A WRONG WAY TO SAY "GOODBYE"?

Maybe some of the relationships in your host nation are so close that you would prefer to stay longer. Perhaps the country with all its nuances has become a second home to you, making you reluctant to leave at all. Unfortunately, your contract is expiring and your company has decided you need to leave. Perhaps the local situation has changed and security, visa issues, work permits, or other factors may keep you from staying. Perhaps personal circumstances (such as education, career, health issues, or aging parents needing support) make it necessary for you to leave.

### YOU ARE LOVING IT...

It may sound strange to others, but maybe you just love everything about your adopted home. Even the traffic jams and unpunctuality of the people. You love the fact that the locals value relationships more than getting the job done timely. Your children feel at home in their schools and have found their way. They have assimilated and have made new friends. Perhaps you or a family member does not want to return to the country you once called "home."

### YOU ARE GLAD...

Another possibility is that you are happy and relieved that you can finally leave. Being the outsider has now come to an end. Sometimes one spouse wants to leave while the other wants to stay. If you have children with you and you were abroad for an extended period, you will usually find yourself with a unique dynamic.

### THE PARENTS' HOME

Taking the step back "home" may seem strange and inappropriate to the children who left with you, regardless of how you as the parent felt in the host nation.

If the home nation is only "home" for the parents and not the children, they will most likely be reluctant to leave. A child who has spent important developmental years abroad understands the host nation to be "home." The child identifies himself with the lifestyle around him. A move is emotionally difficult to process and a child may refuse to say goodbye, often reacting by withdrawing internally or responding with anger, irritation, and other inappropriate outwardly.

As parents you need to recognize this is a normal response. Your child does not have the same connection to the "old home" as you do. Do your best to be empathetic. Explain age appropriately how the decision to move came about. Allow your child to express his or her frustration and anger not only through words, but also through drawing and other creative means. Some children find it very important to express their emotions through movement or touch. Some can release their emotional tension by running and playing, and others might need a punching bag or a back massage.

Some children completely reject the inevitable and instead try to live like before, sometimes even more intensely. In some cases, children may fall into an emotional black hole which may even lead to severe depression.

Should you observe significant social withdrawal or blatant rebellion over the course of a few months, you are advised to seek professional help from a pediatrician or a children's psychologist.

## AVOIDING GOODBYES

Similar reactions are possible with adults. Because so many details need to be attended to prior to the departure, it becomes easy to push your own emotions and hurt aside.

### IF ONE DOES NOT WANT TO LEAVE AT ALL...

Just as it was hard to accept the fact that the time in your host nation is coming to an end, it will also take a while to accept that you are now going to live in your home country again. Those who suppress the thought of saying goodbye will also experience mixed emotions about what they can expect in the homeland. These are not healthy precursors for a new start in the old "home."

If you cannot accept the reality of the farewell, it becomes harder to be open-minded towards your arrival back "home." Those who do not openly handle the emotions and thoughts entwined with the process of saying farewell will find it difficult to transition. Parting is not an easy process, but it is a very important step which needs to be taken intentionally and deliberately.

**TIPS:**

Work experience abroad is worthwhile. Not only do you gain professionally, you experience personal growth in the areas of tolerance, flexibility, and vision.

- Return time should be carefully chosen.
- Good communication with all involved is the key to success.
- Reflect upon the most challenging situations during your previous moves. What caused the most stress?
- Plan together with your spouse and delegate responsibilities according to strengths and individual preferences.
- Include your children age-appropriately in the decision making process.
- Say goodbye in a healthy and thorough way, even if it is not easy.

# The Move

## KING OF CHAOS?

- 40  Loss of Status
- 43  Chaos and Disruption
- 45  The Move—King of Chaos?
- 47  Worries About the Future

Depending upon when you pack your bags, spend your last day at work, get on the plane, and start your new job at "home," the transfer phase can stretch out into an extended period of time. What exactly transpires in the time between the end of your foreign assignment and the new beginning at home?

## LOSS OF STATUS

In the previous chapter you learned that colleagues usually start making plans without you once they hear you are leaving. At your new (maybe even your previous?) work environment in your home country, you have not yet assumed your position. You sit on the fence. In some ways you could even say that you are without status. This is a confusing and unsettling phase when you do not know the ropes anymore.

### AMBIVALENCE

You may feel ambivalent in the situation. It is good to leave as much of a window between ending your old job and starting your new position, for there are still piles to accomplish. The move is both physically and emotionally exhausting. Packing takes time, as well as the goodbye's and later on the hello's as you reestablish relationships with family and friends. On the other hand, "hope deferred makes the heart sick." When the transitional phase between jobs extends months, it may become even more unsettling. It is not really possible to establish new routines for you and your family. Often you are not able to apply your expertise—not anymore and not yet. Since our society places such high value on performance, this phase can be potentially unnerving. You find yourself in the midst of turmoil, both inwardly and outwardly.

**STATUS-FREE**

Being status-free also means that the status you had before moving is non-existent. Many expats enjoy a dynamic, responsible position while they are abroad as they represent their firm or even their nation. Many expats also enjoy a higher level of prestige in their host nation. They are invited to embassy receptions or to the honorary consul. Meetings with the company staff and project managers are routine. They participate in special events with trade organizations and local partners. Wherever he goes, the expat is someone special. People working for non-profits or relief agencies attend meetings hosted by the United Nations or one of their sub-organizations. As an expat, you regularly meet decision makers from all over the world. People recognize you, and you recognize them.

Now you may be heading back to your parent company. You may be accepting a position which gives you much less status in decision making than your position abroad. You may not be getting a promotion, or it may seem the experience you have gained over the past years does not matter. You actually lose status. This humbling turn of events is very difficult for most people to handle.

Even if the return home leads to a step up career-wise or financially, the transitional phase before commencing a new position is confusing and very unsettling.

## THE CHILDREN

In many host nations the children are a novelty simply because they are different than the locals. Depending on your placement, they may be noticed because of their hair or skin color, or perhaps due to an accent, style of dress, or other habits.

Some children enjoyed being driven to school every day by a parent or chauffeur. If your family lived in a more rural area, your children may have had a personal tutor. A local housekeeper may have taken care of laundry and housecleaning details. Maybe she took responsibility for most of the chores like sweeping, setting and clearing the table, and tidying the rooms, not requiring the children to participate in household management.

So many adjustments need to be made upon returning "home." Usually housekeepers, personal tutors, or gardeners are luxuries of the past. The school bus stop is now a dragging ten-minute walk from home.

**SOMETHING TO THINK ABOUT:**

The children are also losing their status.

- In the host nation the children were always "someone special." They have not yet really arrived "at home" and are not sure who they are and how they fit in.
- Many times children feel disoriented and torn between the excitement of something new and the loss of familiarity. Things they had previously taken for granted are now questioned or totally unknown. When this happens, not only do they lose their status, but also a great deal of self-confidence.

## CHAOS AND DISRUPTION

Loss of status alienates and leads to internal turmoil in the returning expat. The chaos of boxes all over the place does not help, either. Somehow, everything is surrounded by uncertainty.

### RELATIONSHIP CHAOS

While relationships are ended in the host nation, new ones are made almost simultaneously in the homeland.

This overwhelming challenge can result in emotional chaos. Returning expats describe they feel isolation, as if they are in a vacuum or "between seats," alone without any real place of belonging.

**TIPS:**

> During the physical transition, between departure and arrival, try to spend a few days in a nice hotel, preferably in another country. A brief time of interlude may reduce some of the emotional stress typically experienced at this time.

### THE CHAOS OF THE UNFINISHED

You have 1001 questions to answer, so many challenges to handle:
- Which moving company should I hire?
- What do I take with me, and what do I leave?
- Where should I, or where do I want to live back "home?"
- What is the easiest way of getting a new vehicle? How do I get rid of the old one?
- What is the best time for shipping my furniture?
- What services need to be canceled and when?
- What needs to be registered and when?
- When should I leave my apartment and move to a hotel?
- Which school is best for my children?
- Will I be able to make new friends quickly?
- What can I expect from my employment?
- What will my relationships with relatives be like?

## THE MOVE—KING OF CHAOS?

**CHECKLIST FOR MOVING**

*3 Months prior*
- Terminate your lease agreement
- Schedule an exact move date
- Organize furniture—What are you taking? Selling? Giving away?
- Look for special offers from moving companies
- End subscriptions, memberships, and contracts with utilities
- Begin slowly preparing children for the upcoming move
- Provide age-appropriate explanation to children
- Investigate new schools and notify current schools of the upcoming move
- Translate and notarize important documents as necessary
- Secure documentation and/or certifications for newly acquired skills
- Educate yourself regarding necessary immunizations and quarantine requirements for any pets
- Plan and schedule experiences and visits with people you still wish to see

*1 Month prior*
- Inform colleagues, friends, and relatives of your new address
- Advise banks, insurance companies, etc. about your move
- Plan a farewell party
- Plan a separate farewell party for your children if appropriate

*2 weeks prior*
- Reconfirm set deadlines with the craftsmen
- Check your energy bill
- Submit a forwarding request at the post office (if possible)
- Pack your boxes and include your children in the process. Things which may seem insignificant to an adult may be meaningful to a child. Ask them if they have any items they want to have easily accessible.

*1 week prior*
- Pack a "survival suitcase" of clothes, medications, and personal hygiene items
- Keep important documents and papers readily accessible
- Plan for intentional breaks. You are only halfway through the journey, as the actual arrival still lies ahead.
- Take time to spend with your children, enjoying the special things in your host country together and building meaningful memories.

Plan for deliberate "routine moments." Even though you are leaving much behind, some things remain. Which processes will be similar in your new daily schedule? Everyone develops a certain routine as to how he starts his day. It may be the daily cup of coffee in bed, or music in the shower. These routines are very personal and may often be maintained during the transition. Many families have bedtime rituals with their children that may include reading a story or saying prayers. Perhaps you have one special date night weekly to enjoy time as a couple. Continuing some of these little personal rituals can add a lot of stability to uncertain times.

Chaos and loss of status can confuse and alienate. You do not know what is going on and sometimes that can be scary. Insecurity and fear are part of the transition and are normal reactions to an abnormal situation. Accept these internal reactions as part of a temporary phase.

## WORRIES ABOUT THE FUTURE

The loss of status and the resulting inner turmoil often result in a dynamic that can cause fear and a low self-esteem.

You are no longer familiar with your surroundings. Lifestyle, relationships, daily routines, and responsibilities change or fall away completely. You begin questioning your own identity. You are not who you used to be, and you are not sure yet who you will be. To most returning expats it feels awkward to lose control of self and circumstances. You may feel alienated and perhaps emotionally insecure.

### EMOTIONAL INSECURITY WITH CHILDREN

Emotional insecurity is easy to recognize with children:
- Increased crying or screaming
- Withdrawing and talking less than usual
- Talking more than usual
- Abiding by rules and established standards seems hard for them
- Demonstrating a rebellious or stubborn attitude
- Regressing in their development (like bed-wetting again)

- Unlearning skills like talking, walking, or eating on their own
- Falling grades or focusing problems in school

### EMOTIONAL INSECURITY WITH ADULTS

Adults may also experience similar symptoms and developments. A married couple recalls:

Carol L.

> "I feel uneasy, agitated, and restless. I have trouble sleeping. I notice that I am experiencing mood swings. Then I find it difficult to be alone, without my friends or husband."

Peter L.

> "Packing the containers, all the logistical issues, the workplace... All of this is just causing me to be frantic. I cannot think straight, I get less done, and I feel as if I hit a wall. I have a thousand thoughts in my head, and yet can hardly accomplish anything. On the inside I feel stressed out and agitated, and somehow I'm becoming insecure."

### EVERYONE REACTS DIFFERENTLY

Our reactions to the increasing stress level during these days, weeks, and months vary. Every adult and every child reacts differently. Are there any useful solutions?

**TIPS:**

Think back to your previous moves.

- What was the hardest part for you?
- How did that affect you emotionally?
- Were you afraid of something? What exactly was it?
- What comforts you in such a situation?
- What helped you deal with the stress? What generally helps you when you are under pressure?
- What strategies could you use currently to reduce your stress levels?

### RECOGNIZING DIFFERENT NEEDS

Just as our reactions to stress are different, so are our needs in these situations. For some people it is important to be able to retreat. That can happen through reading, solving a crossword-puzzle, being creative, or exercising. Others need to be surrounded by people in extremely stressful situations, allowing them to interact. Extroverts find it important to talk through the pent-up stress, whereas introverts prefer to release stress through working crafts, playing music, or writing. Coping strategies are as individual as the people under pressure.

Everyone relies on his own methods for managing stress. People become more self-centered, which is why conflicts—on top of everything else—are inevitable. It becomes necessary to communicate with those close to you—your spouse and children—how the situation has changed you and what your needs are.

The differences in our individual needs can be noticed and valued.

Sandra. M.:

> *"What helps me in those times is talking with others and with my husband, and to take the time to deal with myself. If I get undivided attention and am listened to, then I feel safe, close to my husband, and not as isolated. That makes me happy."*

Mike B.:

> *"What helps me is being able to withdraw—to process things or to be able to go outside for a run."*

Others mention that it helps them to create personal structure and to delegate jobs they do not enjoy. Planning and writing to-do lists is often helpful. It is also important for spouses to be sensitive to each other, to know how the other one is managing and what is keeping him busy, and to understand how they are relating as a couple.

**TIPS:**

Tips for couples and families:
Ask your spouse and your children, "What is the best way for me to support you?"

Moving has the potential of going down in your family history as a time of stress and arguments, an experience you may wish to forget as soon as possible. However, it also has the potential of becoming a special family milestone, something that unites you. It may be a source of strength for your job and everyday responsibilities and something that you may enjoy reflecting upon even a decade from now.

**TIPS:**

Moves stress us out. We lose what had long been safe and familiar. Our reactions and needs become very different.

- Good times with friends or with your spouse and children can help you reenergize and get through the tumultuous time, but those strengthening times do not just automatically happen.
- Everyone loses his status. Ironically, accepting this fact actually fosters security.
- Deliberate quiet times during the transition are helpful.
- Identification of what strengthens and affirms you is crucial.
- What exactly can you do to refuel or reenergize? How often would that activity or process be beneficial?

# Arrival

## HOME, SWEET HOME

- 55 Ten Tips for Surviving After the Return
- 58 Cultural Stress During the Return
- 61 Dealing with Loss and Grief
- 67 Reunions with Colleagues, Friends and Family
- 69 Advice for Superiors, Colleagues, Relatives and Friends
- 76 Challenges for Children and Teenagers

### WELCOME!

Home again! Excellent! At the airport you are welcomed. Family W. returned after spending nine years in Beijing and reminisced about a big welcome banner at the airport.

You receive hugs and welcoming gifts. You are back, and everyone is happy to see you. Your extended family is thrilled by the reunion. Everyone is friendly. Both old and new colleagues want to hear about your experiences, as do your neighbors. Even people in your choir and on your soccer team express interest when seeing you upon your return.

### PREFERABLY ALONE

Some people prefer a quiet return. You do not let anyone know when you are arriving. First, you need a break because the entire process was so disturbing, emotional, and difficult. Perhaps it was unplanned, unwanted, and simply tough. You might not want to see familiar faces at first, and you withdraw. If that works for you, it is perfectly okay.

### WHO IS LISTENING?

How much time do the people who welcomed you so warmly actually grant you? How long do they listen when you are talking about your experiences? Who is actually listening?

Usually your listener is interested only for a very short amount of time. Before you really start your narration, your audience has already moved on. Everyone seems to have a full schedule. Often, the conversation ends with a quick polite,

"Hello, how was..." and your greeter vanishes back into his own world.

Many things may seem strange at first, and some are special. Depending upon where you were, you are grateful for 24-hour hot and cold running water, electricity, and internet connections. The sales at Walmart and Tesco are great, the deals you could only dream of in...

But what happens after the initial excitement is gone?

## TEN TIPS FOR SURVIVING AFTER THE RETURN

The following recommendations are especially helpful during the first year after the return:

### 1. SET REALISTIC GOALS!

It takes time to assimilate into the new situation, especially if you were gone for an extended period of time. Usually returning expats tend to set unrealistic goals with the mindset of, "I know my way around here." That can lead to a constant inner tension.

### 2. TAKE TIME TO OBSERVE!

It is good to have social contacts and to reintegrate quickly. On the other hand, many things have changed. Why do not take some time to observe your surroundings? The rhythm may be completely different than in your host country.

Behaviors which were once familiar to you may now seem a little bit strange.

### 3. ENJOY YOURSELF!

You are discovering new and old things which you enjoy and find relaxing. Maybe you were not able to ride your bike or go running abroad. Some returning expats discover a newfound love for the nature in their home country. Experiencing the cool breeze, the fresh air, the grass that they can walk through carefree with bare feet is all possible again. Hurray!

### 4. PLAN FOR BREAKS!

Please keep in mind that you cannot do everything to perfection. Unfinished tasks often pile up after the arrival. Remember that your body needs enough sleep, which is normal during this transitional phase. Proper nutrition also plays an important role for your overall well-being throughout this difficult time. All the sweets and fast foods available may be tempting at first, but a balanced diet gives your body the strength it needs.

### 5. BE JUST A LITTLE BIT CRAZY!

You were gone for quite a while. You have changed, and that is okay. Things which are normal and acceptable in your hometown may not apply to you anymore. Your experiences and encounters with people from a different culture have changed you. Feel free to come across as a little bit eccentric.

## 6. BE FLEXIBLE!

You may have made a lot of plans for your life back "home." Usually you will not be able to carry them all out. Your actual circumstances are often different than your expectations. Try to be flexible and prepared to tweak your plans. This initial phase is relatively chaotic, and that is normal.

## 7. DO NOT TAKE THE SITUATION TOO SERIOUSLY!

Do not take yourself too seriously. You are bound to make some mistakes while trying to adapt. Just as you did upon arriving in your host nation, you will make mistakes now that you are home. Mishaps happen. If you are able to laugh at yourself in those situations, then you will have come out ahead.

## 8. BE PATIENT WITH YOURSELF!

People back home most likely will not understand your exotic experiences. On the flip side, you often do not understand the others around you. You have to be patient and sensitive. If you show genuine interest in the lives of those back home, reintegration will be easier.

## 9. PRACTICE FORGIVENESS!

If you have made a mistake out of ignorance, forgive yourself. Also be sure to forgive your spouse and your children if they are responsible for an argument. Talk to someone who has also spent time abroad to process your mishaps and the time you dropped the ball with your spouse and children. Sit down together and talk about your week, enjoying some popcorn or ice-cream and a good laugh at the same time.

**10. SHOW GRATITUDE AND ENCOURAGEMENT!**

Being thankful and encouraging is like taking vitamins, especially during your reentry phase. Take your time, laugh at yourself, and do not set your goals too high at the beginning.

> Schedule a medical appointment for a thorough check-up shortly after your return.

Permanent headaches, an upset stomach, irritated skin, or hurting limbs may be signs that you brought a disease back home with you, but they could also be symptoms of extreme stress. Climate change may affect your thyroid. Physical ailments may lead to depressive moods and need to be addressed.

## CULTURAL STRESS DURING THE RETURN

Most people understand that foreign assignments cause cultural stress, but very few expect this same type of stress when returning to their homeland.

The "stress table" by Thomas H. Holmes (see below) does an excellent job illustrating the challenges we face before, during, and after foreign assignments. Holmes' studies prove that an accumulation of more than 300 points within a year lead to an 80% chance of serious health issues during the next year, either physical or psychological.

The returning expat is most likely going to be facing the following stress factors:

**CHECKLIST:**

Stress factors during the foreign assignment:

| Activity | Stress Value |
|---|---|
| • Change in employment | 36 |
| • Change in living standards | 25 |
| • Change in personal habits | 24 |
| • Change in work schedule | 20 |
| • Change in housing | 20 |
| • Change in recreational opportunities | 19 |
| • Change in social activities | 18 |
| • Change in family activities | 15 |
| • Change in diet and nutrition | 15 |
| • Change in language | 50 |
| • Change in financial status | 38 |
| Total points | 280 |

In addition, the following situations cause extra stress:

- Injuries or accidents                          36
- Health problems of a family member             25
- Marital issues                                 24
- Sex issues                                     20
- Change in sleeping patterns                    20

**TIPS:**

Which of these stress factors are you most likely going to face upon your return? You will have to make adjustments.

**RULE OF THUMB**

The more successful you were abroad, the more difficult the return will be for you.

Here is why—If someone is successful in a foreign country, he has adapted very well; however, the behavior learned in the host country does not fit the system back "home."

You must expect cultural stress upon your return. Think of the factors that challenge, upset, and irritate you the most. What can you do to manage them?

## DEALING WITH LOSS AND GRIEF

Remember the famous song by Simon and Garfunkel, "Bridge over Troubled Water"? That's exactly what you need—a bridge built over the waters agitated in you during your transition. This diagram shows how you can safely cross the water.

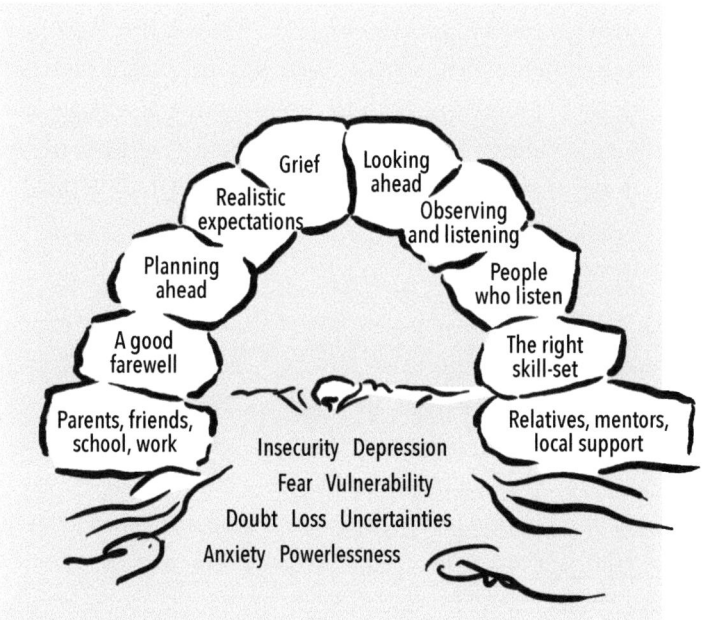

Ideally you are on one side of the bridge—abroad—safe and well integrated. You know your way around and are content and accepted. Healthy relationships with your parents and friends in school, with colleagues, and with a community of like-minded individuals keep you grounded in your host nations.

Now, due to the move, you are standing in front of a rushing river of insecurity, uncertainty, vulnerability, and loss. You are wondering how you are supposed to make it.

The bridge that will successfully bring you across that troubled water is built of several stones. The first stone is a good and positive farewell without any "unfinished business" in our relationships. The next one is planning ahead, which will encourage you and provide perspective as you develop a realistic picture of what is going on in your previous home. You know what to expect, both in regards to the challenges and the opportunities. You also recognize that it is okay to feel loss and it is not necessary for you or your family to hold it together all the time. Grief is normal and important, and it is vital not to suppress it.

Grief. We only grieve if we lost something which was important and meaningful to us. Grief validates something which is gone, and is therefore an important aspect of the process. Everyone grieves differently. How do you express your sadness? How does your spouse? Or your children? Sometimes it is to express in words. Creative arts such as painting can be helpful, and many people find it helpful to write or create a symbol for their loss and grief.

Now look ahead. Take time to listen and observe. Most of us have two eyes, two ears, but only one mouth. As it says in the book of Proverbs, "To answer before listening—that is folly and shame." You can discover a lot of things just by careful observation.

On the other hand it is important to know and meet people who listen to you and understand how you are feeling.

Has anyone in your environment spent an extended period of time abroad or even immigrated from another country? Back "home" you will find these people who understand and support you due to their changed perspective resulting from a foreign assignment a source of encouragement.

In addition to your luggage and some souvenirs, you will bring back a unique skill-set you would like to apply. Which of these skills can you use in your private life? Which can you successfully integrate into your work environment?

Just as your firm supported you by preparing you for your stay in your host culture, it can now support you in your reentry. This can happen with a professional debriefing or through a seminar. Superiors and colleagues who also experience something similar can now be part of an understanding support structure.

Relatives who educated themselves about return dynamics will be empathetic and allow you the time and space necessary for a successful transition, allowing for the best possible reintegration for everyone involved.

**REENTRY COACHING**

The experiences gained abroad are a valuable resource. According to studies conducted by Global Relocation Trends, most returning expats have a strong desire to apply what they have learned and transfer those skills to their current environment. The opinion and support of an expert could be very helpful during this implementation process.

## A NEW WORKPLACE?

Maybe you were sent abroad by your company and can now continue your work within the same corporation. It could also be that you went abroad on a limited contract, working for an outside employment agency or serving in a humanitarian role. Now that you have fulfilled your contract, you will be looking for a new employment upon your return.

The job search can be a long and complicated process for returning expats. An interesting foreign assignment is not always regarded as an asset in your résumé. It is important for you to carefully document all the expertise and skills you acquired abroad, along with your general qualifications.

Many returning expats gained new skills abroad, but regrettably are not able to document them adequately. A detailed portfolio with proof of additional qualifications is very important in your job search. If you do not have certifications for all additional trainings, find out if you are able to secure them now, after the fact.

If you were working for a humanitarian organization, the image that society and potential employers have of your work is very important, especially if you are pursuing a position in an industrial or competitive workplace. HR managers from profit-driven companies tend to be skeptical of applicants who come from the non-profit arena. Make sure you "translate" your skills into a language that is attractive to a profit-driven market. Maybe you gained valuable interpersonal experience, or you were able to considerably improve your logistic skills. Did you learn a new language or strengthen your existing language skills? Are you able to lead negotiations in Spanish or Mandarin? Everything you acquired abroad, often through practical experience, may be used for your application. Reflecting upon and listing all these skills and competencies will also build your self-confidence, a resource which should not be underestimated during an unpredictable and unstable transition.

Of course the current job market and your age play a role when you are looking for employment. It is not uncommon that the end of a foreign contract is followed by temporary unemployment.

**TIPS:**

> The return from a foreign country often leads to a change in employment. Make sure you carefully document all the skills you acquired abroad and are able to communicate them appropriately to your target audience.

## UNEMPLOYMENT

Many firms and organizations prefer to give their employees foreign contracts for their responsibilities overseas, as opposed to a domestic contract. The contract may also be written by a local company. These options are generally more cost effective for the employer. It is important for you to understand that if you had a contract in your host nation that ends with your foreign assignment, you may be unable to claim unemployment benefits.

Unemployment is generally an unpleasant experience for those affected; however, after a return from a foreign assignment, it may also be an opportunity. You are given the time to reorient yourself. It is not imperative you get going right after your arrival, without taking the time to get your bearings again. In the case of unemployment, you absolutely should take time to observe your surroundings. How have the lifestyle and the way people relate with each other changed? What is different about the language and the way people use it? Many things that had been normal are now strange, while things that had seemed odd are now totally accepted. Society and the way people deal with their environment have evolved during your time abroad.

Especially if you were out of the country for an extended period of time, you will notice miscues between you and your peers. Expats tend to adapt their behavior to their host country—often subconsciously—and change some of their old habits.

Use the time offered during your job search to gain new skills or improve those you already have. In this way you can polish the skills and knowledge you gained abroad. You will be wrapping and decorating a package, so to speak.

Keep in mind that your experiences have to make sense and be relevant to a future employer.

Take the time to become clear about your career goals. The majority of returning expats have achieved a very high level of education. Of those working in humanitarian aid, 79% have college degrees, and 21% have specific training within their field. Nearly half of them have completed two certifications, and 62% plan to pursue further vocational training upon their return. These statistics demonstrate a great aptitude for learning and improving oneself.

Together with the passive and documented skills you acquired abroad, you have a great possibility of finding meaningful employment quickly.

Temporary unemployment is often reality when returning from a foreign assignment. Although often considered unpleasant, view this phase as an opportunity to complete unfinished business, develop new skills and qualifications, and define what your goals truly are.

The loss of a good job with intrinsic benefits and a loved home may be sad. Understanding a healthy farewell process is extremely important to weather the storm caused by the move. Take the time to deliberately deal with the feeling of loss.

## REUNIONS WITH COLLEAGUES, FRIENDS AND FAMILY

While you were gone you received significant support and empathy from colleagues, friends, and family. Now, however, you find yourself back home and are not always certain of how to interact. What can help you here?

**CHECKLIST**

- Are there any friends or acquaintances who can understand you because they went through a similar process? Take a few minutes to write down those names.
- Take time in advance to consider your relationships (family, friends, colleagues, and acquaintances) and anticipate how they will react. Will they give you five minutes to share your experiences, or will they show a lot more interest?
- What will you tell your colleagues and acquaintances who cannot relate to your experience? Think of 2-3 sentences they will understand.
- Be prepared for the possibility that you will miss the excitement and motivation that you experienced abroad.
- Support the projects that your colleagues and friends started during your absence.
- Take your time as you work your way back into your social and professional networks.
- Do not plan too much at once. Biting off more than you can chew will likely wear you out, and people who are worn out are more prone to depression.
- Take time to listen to others. If you show interest in the experiences of the people around you, they will most likely want to hear from you.
- Stick to the rules and traditions of your family, friends,

and coworkers. You became very open-minded and flexible through your interaction with people from a different culture, but your contacts at home were not able to benefit from the same experiences.

Who among your colleagues is going to understand you? How long will people listen? What exactly are you going to say?

## ADVICE FOR SUPERIORS, COLLEAGUES, RELATIVES AND FRIENDS

Imagine your colleague, or maybe a friend or relative is returning from abroad. It could be that you are thinking, "He knows his way around. After all, this is his old workplace. He will fit right in within a few weeks."

Unfortunately, things are not quite that easy.

When they return "home," expats often suffer a loss of status and privileges. Even if the return involves a promotion, which is not self-evident, their position loses the significance it had in a foreign culture.

One returning expat recalls:

> "I got invitations from the general consul, from the mayor, and so on. It was just like playing, so to speak, in a different league than in Germany."

## LOSING CONTROL OF THE CIRCUMSTANCES

Generally speaking, a great degree of independence and responsibility is diminished upon returning to the homeland. Knowledge gained and intrinsic skills often do not get recognized and considered. Therefore, reintegration can be a very frustrating process for many returning expats and may lead to numerous conflicts.

## REINTEGRATION DOES NOT HAPPEN AUTOMATICALLY.

For businesses which want to benefit from the international experience of their expats, reintegration is a big challenge.

If this does not work out, the returning expat will hardly be able to incorporate his experiences in a meaningful way. If the employee begins to withdraw and ultimately quits his job, the company loses not only an important staff member, but also valuable know-how and contacts.

Fred S. recalls:

> "When I returned to my old company after eight years abroad, my colleagues who still knew me wanted to know how it was. But they generally were not willing to listen for more than two minutes. They did not really want to know what I had learned."

Three employees had originally signed up for the reentry coaching of a big company in southern Germany. The day of the event, only one showed up.

When he asked about the other two, the reentry coach learned that they had already quit their jobs.

A good support system is worthwhile. How can this actually happen?

- *Listening:* Take the time to listen to the returning expat, even though some of his experiences may sound exotic. Your colleague was probably sought after and prestigious. Now he may feel underestimated and misunderstood.
- *Maximized potential:* Where can your employee apply his experience in the company? He learned extensively while he was out of the country. Try to put that knowledge to achieve company goals. What options do you have here?
- *Language skills:* Maybe your employee communicated in a different language most of the time and gained proficient language skills. How can you benefit?
- *Intercultural sensibility:* Your employee had to adapt to his surroundings in order to face challenges. He learned to understand, and maybe even to supervise, people from a different cultural background. Do you have any personnel from different cultures who could benefit from his skills?
- *Language gaps:* After communicating in a different language for so long, it is normal that initially he may not be able to think of some vocabulary. That is totally normal and can happen multiple times.
- *Expectations:* Speak about mutual expectations as clearly, specifically, and honestly as possible.

### RETURNING EXPATS FEEL NEGLECTED

As a result, many returning expats quit their jobs shortly after they are back. "Businesses lose important insight this way, from people in whom they invested a lot," as Mark Smith from the accounting firm Ernst & Young points out. In the worst case scenario, if employees cannot be successfully integrated, it may lead to "brain drain"—an exodus of highly qualified personnel.

Numerous returning expats feel like Peter G.:

> "Many things have become strange to me, and when I come here for a visit I see the country and the people with a new perspective. And if I hear certain statements or have certain experiences, I am caught off guard much more often than I had been. Before, everything here was normal for me because I did not know any other way. Now, I do not feel at home here any longer. And this is despite the fact it is my language, despite that I appreciate many things here, and despite that I feel homesick at times. I find it hard to imagine my future here."

### HOW REINTEGRATION SEMINARS CAN HELP
- Allow returning expats reflect on gained experiences and manage their personal situation.
- Make them aware of their newly gained skills and help them incorporate new competencies in meaningful ways.
- Provide perspective as to how they are often perceived by others in their workplace and why.

- Identify which behaviors should be avoided in order to facilitate a positive working relationship with colleagues and superiors.
- Match needs and expectations with the future opportunities in the business community.
- Identify which experiences make personal reintegration more difficult, taking into account spouse and children who have moved with you.

Here is what people have to say about reintegration coaching:

> "I thought the reentry coaching and debriefing was very helpful. Afterwards I could look ahead much more relaxed. Thank you!" (I.L., returning from India)

> "It was very important for me." (Dr. J.C., returning from Pakistan)

> "Since the debriefing I feel like I have arrived in Germany." (D.T., returning from Thailand)

> "I think that reentry coaching and debriefing after an intense time abroad should not be missed." (E.W., returning from the United States)

> "Sometimes tiny little things can cause incredible pressure. I did not realize that until they were gone and I literally felt less weight on my shoulders. I never thought that this would be so physically noticeable." (T.G., returning from Haiti)

> "Through your service, you continuously helped both our teams and individual staff members reflect and bring closure to both positive and difficult experiences. This way we experienced firsthand how well you can move on if you have

*reflected well, even after challenging experiences." (J. Fänder, director, YWAM)*

### TIPS FOR RELATIVES AND FRIENDS

Do not be surprised if your loved one suffers from jet lag. He will take some time to adjust. For every hour of time difference, the human body usually requires one day for the inner clock to adjust. Your loved one has changed as a result of his time abroad. His experiences in a different culture have left their mark. The more deeply a person connected with the people and culture of a nation, the more visible these marks can be. Be prepared. Your friend or family member may feel trapped.

Your loved one was able to expand his horizons while he was abroad. He learned there are different ways of approaching things. Now that he is back "home" where things are simply done the way they always have been done, he may feel restricted and trapped. This is not unusual it is a normal reaction. Seminars along the lines of preparation for the transition should be the standard.

Give him some time to adjust to being home again and to any changes in his environment. Do not plan too many events for him upon his return. After the myriad of impressions and experiences abroad, the flight back home and the sudden challenge of being back in the old "home", it is totally normal to feel exhausted.

In a normal conversation, participants balance each other out. They are on the same level. Communication in everyday life works like a seesaw. A constant exchange takes place in an appropriate rhythm. Every partner has something to contribute to a subject. The seesaw goes up and down. Both partners are about equally "heavy" because of their similar experiences.

The unique, or even exotic, experiences of the returning expat turn him into the "fat" person on the seesaw. If you have not been in a similar situation, you cannot "play along." Most people react by saying, "Let me down. This is no fun." They may quickly lose their interest in the conversation.

It is beneficial for both people to keep listening and participating. That way they can work on their relationship and achieve a new, shared level of understanding.

**TIPS:**

In the physical, you are back home. Sometimes this may feel great; sometimes you may feel like running away. Keep in mind:

- Maintain your sense of humor, and forgive both yourself and others. You will need regular times to relax and refuel in order to do so.
- Adolescents need special support during this time.
- Cultural stress during the return transition is normal. Which factors are going to be the most challenging for you? Identify them and think of the best ways to meet them. What irritates you the most? What can you do about that?
- Compose two sentences which you can use to summarize your stay abroad to others.
- Explain clearly to your coworkers how you are doing and why you may no longer understand certain aspects in the work environment.

## CHALLENGES FOR CHILDREN AND TEENAGERS

Children often have the most problems with returning, because their parents' "home" is not necessarily their "home." If the children were not born yet when the parents left and spent their entire life (or an important part of it) abroad, then the host nation became their home. The parents' home may simply be where their grandparents live or where they spend their vacations, but not their home. You need to bear that in mind. The older the children are when they return and the longer they lived abroad, the more challenging the return generally is.

**TIPS:**

> Spend some time together watching prime time TV. Discuss the jokes and expressions you heard, the fashion you saw, and the way people interacted.

## PEER PRESSURE AMONG TEENAGERS

The teen years are a time of big changes in many aspects of life. Until the age of twelve, children depended upon their parents and identified strongly with them. By age 13 or 14, friends mean everything to the teen. The peer pressure is often very intense. Adolescents define themselves and are defined by others through their fashion, their music, their entertainment, and so on. You, as parents, need to bear that in mind both before and during the return. Using the internet as a tool is a big help. Magazines and other media can build a cultural bridge. Current friends or relatives who are (or have children) the same age can give the teen an idea of what is "in" or "out" in his new environment.

Careful observation of people in the new environment will give you much insight. Plan for opportunities to do so, just as you did when you were preparing to move to your host nation.

## AT INCREASED RISK FOR DEPRESSION

Because the important role friends serve for young teens aged 13-15, this seems to be the most risky time for making a major move from one culture to another. The tendency toward depression is especially high in this group. In this developmental stage, teens try to accomplish three things:

1. Define their individuality

2. Find their identity

3. Develop a personal, mature conscience

A stable home, one from which a teen is able to leave to test things out and then confidently return to a place of safety and security, is extremely important for a teen. In this developmental phase common stress reactions to moving include escape into fantasy, withdrawal, or rebellion.

In the worst case scenario, teenagers can become very destructive or even delinquent.

Teens are usually not aware of their dynamics. They often find themselves in a whirlwind of emotions that they cannot explain or understand. They may feel anger because it was not their choice to leave, or insecurity because they do not always know what is going on, or fear because they do not know their way around and are not sure how things will turn out.

This is why reintegration seminars are especially important for teenagers.

## BURNOUT AND DEPRESSION

Burnout and depression are not rare among returning children, adolescents and adults, but they can usually be prevented under the following conditions:

- They may "unload" emotionally. They need to access their own emotions. A supportive environment where adolescents do not internalize conflicts too long will help during these troubled times.
- They learn to say, "No." Often children and teens get overwhelmed with offers for sports and recreational activities. Expectations and demands from relatives in the home country can be a real challenge. Setting boundaries to provide stability and security creates more freedom.
- You are aware of your own feelings, especially feelings of despair and fear.
- It is completely normal to be overtaken by these emotions in the return phase. Take a break if this happens, and recognize these feelings as part of the return process.
- You follow a nutritious and healthy diet.
- You take time for fellowship and nurture relationships with people who are important to you. You can laugh and relax. "A happy heart is the best medicine." A fun evening with your friends or family can ease the tension.

- You schedule regularly for athletics and fitness. Exercise is proven to produce endorphins in your body which will make you feel better emotionally.
- You get enough sleep.
- You nurture your soul. Slow down when confronted with challenges and focus on your inner goals. This can also happen through prayer and meditation or participating in a church service.

Children often have the most problems with returning. The parents' home is usually not their home. Accept this fact. Give them time and allow them to be sad. Above all, listen!

The following table illustrates well the phases that children, adolescents and adults go through during a cultural move.

# THE TRANSITION EXPERIENCE

*The Transition Experience,* David C. Pollock, *Interaction Inc.*

| SOCIAL STATUS | SOCIAL POSTURE | PSYCHOLOGICAL EXPERIENCE | TIME ORIENTATION |
|---|---|---|---|

## 1. INVOLVEMENT

| BELONGING | COMMITTED | INTIMACY | PRESENT ORIENTED |
|---|---|---|---|
| Part of 'in' group<br>Reputation<br>Position<br>Knowing | Responsible<br>Responsive | Confirmed<br>Secured | |

## 2. LEAVING

| CELEBRATING | DISTANCING | DENIAL | FUTURE/ TEMPORARY |
|---|---|---|---|
| Attention<br>Recognition<br>Farewells<br>Closures | Loosen ties<br>Relinquish roles<br>Disengage | Rejection<br>Resentment<br>Sadness, Guilt<br>Anticipation (expectations) | |

## 3. TRANSITION

| STATUSLESS | CHAOS | ANXIETY | FUTURE |
|---|---|---|---|
| Unknown<br>Lack of structure<br>Special knowledge without use | Must initiate relation-<br>  ships, Isolation<br>Self-centered<br>Exaggerated problems<br>Ambiguity/<br>  misunderstanding | Loss of self-esteem<br>Loss of continuity/sacred objects<br>Grief from loss<br>Emotional instability<br>Dreams, Disappointment<br>Panic | |

## 4. ENTERING

| INTRODUCING | SUPERFICIAL | VULNERABILITY | PRESENT/ TEMPORARY |
|---|---|---|---|
| Marginality<br>Mentor searching<br>Uncertain of position/<br>  response<br>Misinterpretation of<br>  behavior-signals | Observer<br>Uncertain of trust<br>Exaggerated behavior<br>Risk taking<br>Search for mentor<br>Errors in response | Fearful<br>Ambivalent<br>Easily offended<br>Depression<br>Psychological problems | |

## 5. RE-INVOLVEMENT

| BELONGING | COMMITTED | INTIMACY | PRESENT/ PERMANENT |
|---|---|---|---|
| Known<br>Knowing<br>Position | Belonging<br>Involved<br>Conforming behavior<br>Concern for others | Secure<br>Affirmed | |

# Reintegration

**FINDING YOUR PLACE**

85   Back Home: The Importance of Reflection

89   What Did I Bring Along?

91   How Long Does Reintegration Take?

98   Phases of Reintegration

96   What About the Children?

101   Truly Reintegrated

Very likely you will feel foreign, lost, and in the wrong place at some point after your return. This is why it is important to plan for some extra time. Daily obligations start coming in quickly for you as a returning expat. Many details need to be managed, and important tasks begin piling up quickly.

An old story from Africa describes a journey. At that time it was common to hire carriers to haul important items pieces of luggage through the jungle. A group of western travelers had also hired carriers. After the first exhausting day of their journey through the jungle, they sat down at the fire in the evening and realized that they had made significantly more progress than expected.

The next morning the western travelers got up early to continue their journey at the previous day's rapid pace.

The locals, however, sat around the campfire for hours. When they still had not moved by noon, the white men became impatient and pushed them to leave. One of the native men looked at them and said, "We walked so fast yesterday, our soul has not been able to follow yet. We are waiting for it to catch up, and then we can leave."

Allow your soul time to arrive. Take time to pause, reflect, and express what you have experienced.

## BACK HOME: THE IMPORTANCE OF REFLECTION

You experienced a lot abroad. These experiences can enrich your life and future and release newfound energy. They can also provide you with new perspectives. This does not, however, happen spontaneously.

### REFLECT TO RECONNECT

After your return you may be tempted to jump back into various activities. Actually, many things will need to be taken care of—vocational challenges, details with government agencies, enrollment in new schools, visits to relatives, etc. Plan ahead for a deliberate break.

Your foreign experience can be compared to a rich, hearty meal. A good meal is supposed to reenergize you, enabling you to tackle your next task successfully. To accomplish that, you must chew carefully and digest properly. It is unhealthy to simply gulp down the meal and quickly carry on. You will feel bloated and tired, get hiccups, and maybe even pass gas. The meal cannot serve its purpose anymore—to reenergize you.

As Hans Menning explains in his book "Das psychische Immunsystem" (Hofgrefe, 2015): "...through reminiscing the past is brought into order, and events can be interpreted positively or negatively. Through reflection new aspects can be discovered, giving an event a new, unexpected meaning. This clarity prevents regret from settling in and unfolding its psycho-toxic effect. The psyche is enhanced by one more immune defense as another psycho-pathogen is neutralized."

**TIPS:**

We call this reflection debriefing. A debriefing includes:

- Reducing emotional and physical stress
- Preventing burnouts
- Accelerating the transition process
  Debriefing helps you breathe deeply so you may engage with newfound energy.

A debriefing also has the following advantages:

**VERBALIZE**

Expressing your thoughts and emotions brings clarity. It helps you gain another perspective and organize your experiences internally. While talking to another person, you may receive insight and understanding of which you were not previously aware.

**NORMALIZE**

Returning expats often find their own reaction to unusual situations very intense or even extraordinary. When they reflect in a group they realize that they are not the only person who is feeling this way. The same goes for the family. By reminiscing and reflecting together, everyone involved will find that they share similar feelings with the others. This process allows your own perceptions to be put into context. They are common reactions to uncommon situations.

## CONTEXTUALIZE

A good debriefing will help you to put your experiences into context with your life as a whole. It helps you discover your future goals and ambitions, and helps identify prior dreams which are no longer important.

After the return a lot of things may seem strange to you. Take some time, together with an independent reentry professional, to reflect upon your time abroad and your departure.

A debriefing can also be compared to the work in a library. Imagine a new book—a weighty volume—landing on the librarian's desk. Now it is the librarian's job to open the book, peruse it, and get a synopsis. What kind of book is this? To which genre does it belong? Is it a love story, a novel, science fiction, or a nonfiction book? The book gets categorized, cataloged, and numbered before it can be shelved. This process makes it easy to find and use the ingredients if necessary. Until the librarian has completed the job of categorizing, cataloging, and numbering the book, it has to remain on the desk. As long as it is there, it blocks the space for newly arriving books.

It seems that people find it hard to simply "put away" an experience abroad without first reflecting upon it carefully. A good reflection makes it easier to move on. It also becomes easier to face new challenges and to retrieve the "book" from the shelf if it seems it will be useful.

One important building block of this reflection is to become aware of skills and changes in our values.

## WHAT DID I BRING ALONG?

You probably brought a suitcase back home with you, or maybe you even shipped an entire container. You may bring out some treasures—a vase from China or a sombrero from Mexico. Ask yourself which invisible treasures you brought along.

### WHICH INNER TREASURES DID YOU BRING?

A practical and creative exercise will help you to reflect, write down and verbalize what became important to you during your time abroad. Thereafter you can ask yourself how you can apply these "treasures" in your home nation. Sometimes it is helpful, if others ask, "How exactly do you envision implementing this?"

### EXAMPLES

*In the area of personal development:*
- I am now fluent in Arabic; I want to continue giving presentations in Arabic.
- My understanding of other cultures increased; I want to approach foreign people around me with more appreciation.

*In the vocational area:*
- I had room for improvement in my organizational skills and received much support, despite my lack of experience before I came; I want to encourage and support young staff members.
- I received encouraging, positive feedback from others; I want to compliment colleagues more than I criticize.

*In the area of family:*
- We rediscovered how valuable it is spending time together; we will schedule regular family days, just for us.
- Etc.

You will most likely also recollect some unpleasant or difficult experiences. Maybe you did not feel accepted or were not taken seriously on your team. Now you can decide what you want to do with that kind of experience. The Austrian neurologist and psychiatrist as well as Holocaust survivor and founder of Logotherapy, Viktor E. Frankl, speaks of the "Trotzmacht des Geistes", the power of the human spirit to say "but". We are able to draw positive conclusions from negative experiences. We humans have received the capability to say, "Yes, I was not taken seriously or accepted; nevertheless, I still want to be the person who takes others seriously and accepts them."

**TIPS:**

Think about what exactly you brought home with you next to souvenirs.

- Specific professional knowledge
- A changed world view
- Interpersonal knowledge and experience
- Familiar experiences

## HOW LONG DOES REINTEGRATION TAKE?

Depending upon how long you were gone from home, your reintegration will take between six and twelve months. If the foreign assignment was over a period of years, then the reintegration process may also take years. It is not until the process is complete that you will be able to say, "I am at home here again." After experiencing a year with all its seasons and celebrations, you will feel more secure and more at home.

Another factor which comes into play is to what degree you did strike camp before you moved abroad. Did you give up your apartment and your workplace?

Will you have to move in with your parents or other family members after you return? If so, than the return process may be more difficult.

The reintegration process extends a minimum of one year, and often longer if the foreign assignment lasted for a number of years.

## PHASES OF REINTEGRATION

Most returning expats go through different phases during their return and reintegration.

### 1. THE TOURIST PHASE

If you for example are returning from a developing or third-world country, it is a pleasure to have running water again and not need to disinfect fruits. Supermarkets have everything your heart desires, you do not need to negotiate prices, and you understand (nearly) everything. You smell familiar food again and listen to sounds you missed while being abroad. Family and friends are excited to have you back and offer their assistance in your everyday life. When you share your experiences, they listen.

You are the center of attention. Everything has a certain glow and brings you joy. Unfortunately, this phase comes to an end and is followed by…

### 2. THE DISILLUSIONMENT PHASE

At some point you realize that you do not know the rules of the game anymore. You feel somewhat disoriented. Having packed your boxes before the departure, you are now engaged in a game of Hide and Seek with your belongings. The situation can be chaotic. The joy of being home again vanishes. Frustration kicks in. Things that seemed normal to you now feel exaggerated. You see the ones who stayed as cold-hearted because they start losing interest in your experiences. All these factors lead to disillusionment.

### 3. THE ALIENATION PHASE

You do not really want to have anything to do with these cold-hearted, narrow-minded people and begin to withdraw. The feeling of being in the wrong place becomes stronger, and you begin to feel isolated and alienated.

Your friends keep their distance, because they fear they will be overwhelmed with your "great" experiences. The feeling of not being able to talk to anyone grows in you, often leading you to become judgmental.

### 4. THE JUDGMENTAL PHASE

You do not understand why no one has time for you. The people in your circle may feel inferior and less talented, so they start avoiding your presence. On the flip side, you begin seeking contact with people who have had similar experiences or to those from other cultures.

### 5. THE SETBACK PHASE

You can consider it a setback if you simply dive headlong into your previous responsibilities and ways, acting as if you had never left. You are thereby denying the significant internal metamorphosis you experienced.

### 6. THE FLIGHT AND SEPARATION PHASE

An unprocessed return can lead to many different ailments, including various physical symptoms, sleeping disorders, and depression. The emotional turmoil can tear you up on the inside and cause you to lose perspective for your future; however, it really does not have to come that far.

When you return, it is normal to go through the tourist, the disillusionment, and the alienation phases, but no one needs to become judgmental. That choice is up to you.

### YOU ARE NOT THE SAME PERSON ANYMORE

A successful reintegration is characterized by the realization that you have changed and will never fit in "at home" as you did before your departure. At the same time you decide to incorporate your new skills and your changed state of mind in both your social circles and your work environment.

How well and how fast you reintegrate back "home" depends on four aspects of life. These can be explained on a hierarchical pyramid.

**ORGANIZATION**

**CULTURE**

**RELATIONSHIPS**

**SKILLS AND HABITS**

Every aspect can be shown depicted on a spectrum. Carefully examine every spectrum and estimate your personal well-being. You can mark the statement on the spectrum which most accurately describes your current state of mind.

**WORKLOAD**
overwhelming ··············································· fulfilling

**SOCIAL CONTACTS**
isolated ··············································· integrated

**HEALTH**
sick ··············································· healthy

**IMPORTANT RELATIONSHIPS**
complicated ··············································· encouraging

**FAMILY INTEGRATION**
frustrating ··············································· strengthening

**CULTURAL SKILLS**
insecure ··············································· secure

**LIFE CRISES**
distressing ··············································· managed

**POSITION IN THE FIRM**
certain ··············································· uncertain

**RELATIONSHIPS IN THE WORKPLACE**
demanding ··············································· supportive

**STRESS-MANAGEMENT**
overwhelming ··············································· relaxed

**PERSONAL HABITS**
not good ··············································· good

Now ask yourself the following questions:
- In what area do you have the most resources?
- How can you maintain and strengthen these?
- Which area is currently your weakest?
- What can help you facilitate positive change?

If you are in a relationship, both partners may complete this self-evaluation. Afterwards you can compare the results and brainstorm what action steps to take. These questions may also be answered by children.

It is expected that in this rebuilding phase you are not living and working "at full speed ahead," but it is important that you do not run empty in several areas.

After returning from abroad you experience different phases. Accept the fact that you have changed and show openness, interest and the will to reintegrate.

## WHAT ABOUT THE CHILDREN?

Children who grew up abroad will never be completely like children that always lived in one culture. They are Third Culture Kids (TCKs), and they will remain Third Culture Kids.

> "I am not a tree that is planted firmly in one spot and develops deep roots. I am a cloud. A cloud is made out of water. It can have different shapes. Sometimes it is moved by the wind in the sky, and sometimes it unites with other clouds. Then it rains down and becomes part of a lake. Other times it turns to snowflakes and covers the world in white. I like that!"

This is how a young woman felt who spent a significant portion outside of her parents' home nation. Within the home she was raised in her parents' culture, but as soon as she opened the front door she was immersed in the culture of her host nation. She understood the values and views of both cultures and from that developed a third culture, resulting in her label as a *Third Culture Kid* (TCK).

> "A TCK is a person who spent an important part of their developmental years outside the culture of the parents. A TCK builds relationships to all cultures, without fully conforming to any single one. Even though elements from multiple cultures are part of the TCK's life experience, they identify with people from a similar background."
>
> David Pollock and Ruth van Reken

## WHAT DOES IT ACTUALLY MEAN TO BE A TCK?

TCKs are adaptable, like chameleons. In your culture of origin it may be normal to look people in the eye and shake hands. In Southeast Asia this is not normal and is considered impolite. Children with British or Swedish parents for example who grow up in Thailand learn to see both behaviors as normal and correct, without fully belonging to either culture. If you were to ask TCKs where they feel at home, they will not be able to name one specific place. Home is connected to relationships, usually where the family is.

Alex Graham James describes his identity as a third culture and his inner turmoil:

> *"I am a confusion of cultures. Uniquely me.*
>
> *I think this is good because I can understand the traveler, sojourner, foreigner, the homesickness that comes.*
>
> *I think this is also bad because I cannot be understood by the person who has sown and grown in the same place. They know not the real meaning of homesickness that hits me now and then.*
>
> *Sometimes I despair of understanding them. I am an island and a United Nations.*
>
> *Who, but God, can recognize either in me?"*

### POSSIBILITIES AND CHALLENGES FOR A TCK

The challenge for TCKs is to find and define their own roots. They always describe home as "somewhere else" or "I do not know." Third Culture Kids are able to adapt everywhere, without ever really feeling at home. It is family connections which bring them stability. They often find it difficult to make decisions. Important decisions in the past often were linked to farewells. In most cases, their parents made decisions for the whole family. TCKs often experienced that they had little input in the decisions made. When those decisions were made, they often changed a big part of their environment. Therefore, TCKs naturally become hesitant about making decisions. At the same time, children and teenagers who grew up abroad find it hard to make long-term commitments. So many things in their worlds have changed significantly time and time again. Family and relationships among other TCKs are especially meaningful. Of course every person is different, and TCKs stress how important it is to them not to be categorized and to be understood as individuals.

The following characteristics need to be understood in the context of the personality and environment in which a person grew up.

"Where I am today is only temporary." TCKs rarely settle permanently. Due to the mobility in which they lived—but rarely chose—TCKs are adaptable and self-confident in new situations. Some TCKs also react in the opposite way to their non-chosen mobility. They never want to move again. TCKs know people from many nations with whom they shared a chapter of their life. They as well as many of their friends moved often. There always was a level of fluidity in their social circles. They develop deep connections in short periods of time. They often value intense and honest relationships. On the other hand, some do not like to start new relationships out of fear of having to say goodbye again soon.

If they suffer painful losses, they tend to let go of the pain quickly. The pain of saying goodbye is too great. However, where pain gets pushed aside, it is also difficult to experience real joy.

Although saying goodbye is part of routine life for TCKs, it does not make it easier for them. Facilitated discussions such as a debriefing can be a good support for them. Both children and adults need time to mourn.

Since it is often painful to let someone go again, TCKs may start to withdraw.

TCKs have the advantage of speaking at least two languages. That, however, brings to question which is the mother tongue. It is not necessarily the language of the parents. Which language do they speak the most? Oftentimes, it is English, because many attend international schools. They may also go to a local school and speak the language of their host nation. But what happens when they return to their home country? Do they perhaps speak with a very different accent?

TCKs know that the world does not end with the country's border. Their horizons often stretch farther than those of their peers. In their home nation they also often seem more mature.

Cultures show in our values—what we perceive as normal, how we describe our lives and habits, and how we think. Or as Myron Loss once put it "Culture is what makes you a stranger when you are away from home."

TCKs reflect a mixture of different cultures. They may look British, but act Australian or Thai. They often cannot identify with the culture in their home nation. Jessica L. daughter of a German couple who grew up in Brazil says, "Germans are stupid! They are always so serious and strict. They do not understand humor and rarely laugh." TCKs can identify with more than one culture, and for that reason they stick out in their home country with their different way of thinking and lifestyle. They feel most comfortable when they are around other TCKs. They are well prepared for a global market.

These resources can often be used for a work position, regardless if the employment is in a social or administrative field, in the sciences, or in a craft. Very few western businesses are without an international focus in regards to both their staff and their practices. Knowledge of these skills and acceptance of them are prerequisites for applying them successfully.

Children who have spent multiple years of their life abroad are different, which is both enriching and challenging.

## TRULY REINTEGRATED

True reintegration is marked by the realization that you have changed during your time abroad. Oftentimes you think differently now. You accept that you will never fit into your home culture as you have before. At the same time you become more willing to accept and appreciate the people back home, even if they do not react as you hoped they would.

When you nurture this attitude, it will have a positive effect on your relationships with the people who stayed at home while you were abroad. Now you will be ready and free to have new experiences and encounters. You will bring your international experiences to your job and social circles. The process of reintegration begins to work.

The changes experienced during the return often result in the pain of separation and an inner sadness. They serve as harbingers for the end of a chapter in our life. At the same time they are a major opportunity to integrate all that has been learned into the future and become the challenging beginning of a new chapter. Only those who face the pain of parting and the sadness that comes with letting go of the familiar, the special memories, and habits are able to embrace new ones. Accept this challenge and start a new and also exciting chapter in your life.

**TIPS:**

Reintegration after a foreign assignment does not happen automatically.

- Take your time to reflect. Consider booking a debriefing and reentry coaching with a professional and neutral facilitator.
- Ask yourself, what treasures did I bring back from abroad.
- Be aware that reintegration is a process, beginning with a decision.
- And: Make sure to allow yourself time for the reintegration process.

## ABOUT THE AUTHORS

Jochen and Christine Schuppener are a German couple who spent eight years abroad with their three children. As training managers in England and Southeast Asia, they prepared, equipped and supported multi-national teams for their deployments.

The authors work freelance as coaches and consultants for international businesses and various non-profit organizations. Their clients work worldwide in more than 100 countries.

Jochen and Christine Schuppener also lecture at multiple educational facilities. Their main focus is intercultural human resources management and coaching—from sending to reintegration—as well as international team development.

### CONTACT

Jochen & Christine Schuppener
Intercultural Coach M.A. &
*Team Management Systems*™ Consultant
Government certified Expatriate Adviser (AusWG)
Psychological Consultant & Personal Coach
Berliner Ring 35 b
86916 Kaufering
Germany
info@schuppener-global-transitions.com
www.schuppener-global-transitions.com